LinguiSystems'

Blooming RECIPES ™

Fun Recipes for Serious
Language Enrichment
Based on
Bloom's Taxonomy

Carolyn S. Tavzel
and the staff of
LinguiSystems

LinguiSystems Inc.
3100 4th Avenue
East Moline, IL 61244

ISBN # 1-55999-028-7

1-800-ALL TIME   In Illinois, 1-800-851-8237   Outside the U.S.,   309-762-5112

Table of Contents

About the Authors

Carolyn S. Tavzel, M.A., CCC is a Speech-Language Pathologist for the Orange County School System in Orlando, Florida. *Blooming Recipes* is her first publication with LinguiSystems.

Seven Speech-Language Pathologists of the LinguiSystems' Staff teamed with Carolyn to write *Blooming Recipes*: Linda Zachman, Mark Barrett, Rosemary Huisingh, Carolyn Blagden, Jane Orman, Barbara Walter, and Kamala Simonton.

August 1987

Introduction

How do we learn language? From the day we are born, we develop our language and thinking skills by listening, watching, and experiencing our environment. Through this firsthand experience, we learn new vocabulary and learn how to categorize, associate, and compare. In fact, according to Bloom, "experience is the best teacher."

Who is Bloom and what does he say about learning? Benjamin S. Bloom is a well-respected researcher in the field of education. His ideas about effective ways to teach, presented in his book, Taxonomy of Educational Objectives* (1956), form the basis for many educational programs. A basic outline of his theory is presented in the following chart.

Thinking Skill Levels	Descriptions	Goals
KNOWLEDGE	Your child can recall bits of information.	to learn basic facts and information; to remember information long enough to answer simple questions about it
COMPREHENSION	Your child can understand information given, but cannot yet relate it to other material.	to demonstrate knowledge by describing or explaining events in his own words
APPLICATION	Your child can use what he already knows in new situations.	to use previously learned knowledge to solve problems in new situations
ANALYSIS	Your child can break a whole into its parts.	to take a situation apart, list the components, and discuss how it was done
SYNTHESIS	Your child can put parts together to form a new whole.	to compare the relationships among ideas and situations; to abstract from previous knowledge to form new or creative ideas
EVALUATION	Your child can state his opinions and give reasons.	to state opinions and infer emotions given the situation; to justify answers

*Benjamin S. Bloom, *Taxonomy of Educational Objectives* (New York, New York: Longman, Inc., 1956).

What are Blooming Recipes? *Blooming Recipes* are a collection of fun, easy recipes you can use to stimulate and enrich the language skills of your young children. Making things together promotes language usage in a very natural setting. Children have more fun learning language in this way, and they are more likely to use the new language again in other situations.

How are the recipes organized? There are twenty-five easy-to-follow recipes to experience with your youngsters. Each recipe provides a list of the ingredients and the utensils needed, as well as step-by-step directions for making the dish. Following each recipe are a list of the vocabulary you use while fixing the recipe, a description of related language activities, a section for writing follow-up remarks and ideas, and sample discussion questions. These questions are arranged in a hierarchy of increasing complexity based on the teaching ideas of Bloom.

How do I use the recipes to teach language? Make the recipe with your children, using the questions provided as a springboard for discussion. Ask your questions before, during, or after each recipe, whichever is most natural for you and your youngsters. Sample answers have been provided for each question except for those questions at the level of Evaluation. (At this level, answers vary too greatly to be easily sampled.) Any time a question is answered with one word, encourage your children to explain their answers as much as possible. Feel free to encourage any correct responses in addition to the samples provided. Also, note that the thinking levels overlap in many respects. It is not crucial to ask all questions in a given level in sequence before proceding to the next level. Normal interaction will usually blend questions across levels in a dynamic, shared experience with the children.

Use the space following "Zesty Extras" to write in any comments or suggestions you want to share with parents, teachers, or others. Indicate any vocabulary words the child needs to practice, as well as any notes about the child's particular experience in making the recipe with you.

Special Considerations:

The number of servings for each recipe is not specified. Since amounts will vary greatly depending upon the ages of the children involved, their tastes, and how the activity is conducted, use your own judgment in each case to determine the quantity to make.

Some of the recipes involve cutting with sharp knives. To insure safety, have the children watch while you do the cutting or let them help by placing their hands over yours.

Suggestions for Classroom Use:

You may want to break the class into several smaller groups and have them take turns making the recipe. After all the groups have finished, lead a discussion with the entire class.

Suggestions for Home Use:

Blooming Recipes are appropriate for Mom, Dad, or older sister or brother to do with any young family member. These activities can be used as follow-up to work at school or as activities to do for the first time at home. Just remember to experiment, keep it natural, and keep it fun.

Remember, these *Blooming Recipes* are not meant as a program, but are meant to be a group of semi-structured activities that provide a fun framework for language learning. To offer the richest learning experience, let your children take the lead as much as possible. Have them gather the materials needed. Allow them to make a mess, change the recipe, and make guesses in "what might happen if" situations. The key things to remember are:

- keep the conversation free-flowing,

- sprinkle your comments with descriptive words and repetition as a language model, and

- use generous amounts of positive reinforcement.

Nothing encourages learning more than fun, so all you teachers, speech-language clinicians, and parents, go ahead and select one of these simple but fun recipes, add some children, mix well, and ENJOY!

Tangy Lemonade

Ingredients:

¼ cup sugar
¼ cup water
2 lemons
several ice cubes

Utensils:

glass
juicer
measuring cup
paring knife
spoon
strainer

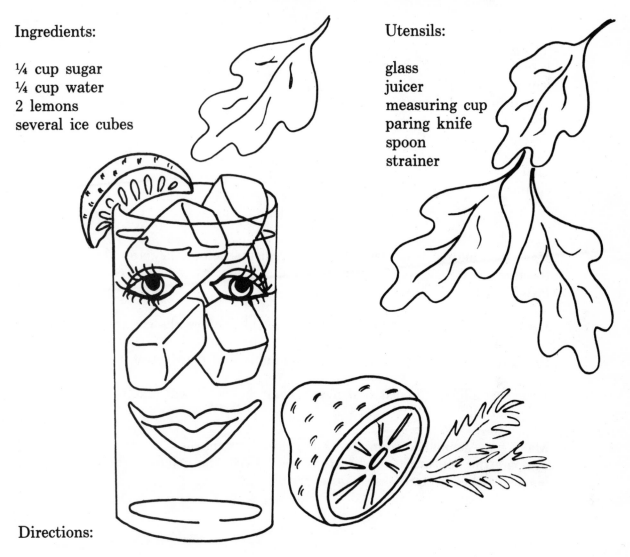

Directions:

1. Pour the sugar and the water into the glass.

2. Stir the sugar and water together until the sugar is dissolved.

3. Cut the lemons in half with the paring knife.

4. Squeeze the lemons on the juicer until you have ⅓ cup of lemon juice.

5. Strain the lemon juice into a measuring cup.

6. Add the lemon juice to the sugared water.

7. Stir the mixture.

8. Add the ice cubes and serve. What a refreshing drink!

5

Tangy Lemonade

Vocabulary:

Nouns	Verbs	Modifiers
juicer	add	dissolved
lemon	cut	fresh
lemon juice	pour	half
measuring cup	serve	several
mixture	squeeze	sour
paring knife	stir	sugared
rind	strain	sweet
seed		
spoon		

Activities:

Have the children taste each of the ingredients before they are added together. Ask how each ingredient tastes. Then, ask whether each ingredient tasted good by itself.

Use a transparent glass to make the lemonade. Have the children observe as the sugar and water are mixed together. Then, talk about what happened to the sugar. Use the word *dissolved*, explaining and demonstrating its meaning.

Have the children predict how many lemon halves it will take to make ⅓ cup of lemon juice.

Make some lemonade from frozen and powdered mixes. Let the children compare the appearance and taste of each. Ask the children which kind of lemonade they prefer, fresh or prepared.

Zesty Extras:

Tangy Lemonade

Blooming Questions:

Knowledge

Name the ingredients we used to make the lemonade. *sugar, water, lemons, ice cubes*
What did we dissolve in water? *sugar*
What did we use for stirring? *spoon*
What did we use to squeeze the lemons? *juicer*

Comprehension

Tell how we made the lemonade. *See the recipe.*
Describe a lemon. *yellow, citrus fruit, has seeds, tastes sour, has juice*
Name something we used that's sharp. *paring knife*
What did we use the strainer for? *to keep the seeds and pulp out of the lemon juice*

Application

What other things can be dissolved in water? *instant coffee, honey, salt, etc.*
What other containers could we have mixed the lemonade in? *pitcher, large cup, mug*
Name some other sour foods. *green apples, grapefruit, limes*
Name some other sweet foods. *honey, peaches, candy*

Analysis

Why did we put sugar in the lemonade? *to sweeten it*
How are sugar and lemons alike? *both foods*
How are they different? *sugar is sweet, lemon is sour*
What makes the lemonade taste sweet? *sugar*

Synthesis

What could we add to the lemonade for decoration? *lemon slice, mint leaves, fancy straw*
Why is it important to use fresh lemons? *more vitamins, stronger flavor*
What could we use instead of sugar? *honey*
Tell what we could do if the lemonade was too sour. *Add more sugar.*

Evaluation

When would be a good time to make this recipe?
What could we do to make the lemonade taste better?
What was the easiest part of making the lemonade?
What was the hardest part?

7

Citrus Knockout

Ingredients:

1 12-ounce can frozen orange juice, thawed
1 12-ounce can frozen lemonade, thawed
6 cups cold water
1 bottle ginger ale, chilled

Utensils:

cups
ladle
measuring cup
punch bowl

Directions:

1. Pour the thawed orange juice and lemonade into the punch bowl.

2. Add the water.

3. Stir the ingredients with the ladle.

4. Just before serving, pour the ginger ale into the mixture and stir with the ladle.

5. Pour into cups.

6. Serve and enjoy!

Citrus Knockout

Vocabulary:

Nouns	*Verbs*	*Modifiers*
bottle	pour	before
ginger ale	serve	chilled
ingredients	stir	citrus
ladle		frozen
measuring cup		thawed
mixture		
ounce		
punch		
punch bowl		

Activities:

Have the children look at the frozen juice concentrates before and after they are thawed. Have them describe the appearances of the frozen and thawed juices. Discuss why it is necessary to thaw the juices before putting them in the mixture.

Have the children taste each of the ingredients before you mix them together. Have the children compare the different tastes.

Have the children taste the mixture at room temperature, and the normal chilled version. Ask the children to compare the two versions and tell which one they prefer.

Plan a party with citrus punch on the menu. Have the children pick some other foods and drinks that would be good to serve with the punch.

Zesty Extras:

Citrus Knockout

Blooming Questions:

Knowledge

What is the name of this punch? *Citrus Knockout*
How many cups of cold water did we use? *six*
Tell what we did with the ginger ale. *poured it into the mixture just before serving*
What utensils did we need to make this recipe? *punch bowl, ladle, measuring cup, and cups*

Comprehension

Tell how to make Citrus Knockout. *See the recipe.*
What does *chilled* mean? *kept cold or cool without freezing*
Describe a ladle. *a deep-bowled, long-handled spoon used for serving liquids*
Describe a punch bowl. *large bowl, usually glass*

Application

Why did we thaw juices? *so they would pour easily into the mixture*
How could we keep the punch cold after we made it?
   put it into the refrigerator or put ice cubes in it
Fix this silly sentence: Oranges, lemons, and bananas are citrus fruits.
   Oranges, lemons, and limes are citrus fruits.
What is one word for a ladle and a measuring cup? *utensils*

Analysis

How are orange juice and lemonade alike? *Both are juices made from fruits.*
How are they different? *Orange juice is made from oranges, but lemonade is made from lemons.*
Why do we need ginger ale in this recipe? *to add carbonation, or sparkle, and flavor*
What could we use instead of a ladle? *wooden spoon, teaspoon, stirrer, etc.*
What was the first thing we had to do for this recipe? *thaw the frozen juices*

Synthesis

Make up your own punch recipe. What kind of fruit juices would you use? *Answers will vary.*
What would you call your punch recipe? *Answers will vary.*
Why do we need to add the ginger ale just before serving?
   to make sure it's fizzy when people drink it
Draw a special way to serve citrus punch for a party. *Answers will vary.*

Evaluation

What is your favorite kind of punch?
Tell how you would convince a friend that Citrus Knockout is the best drink you've ever tasted.
Is Citrus Knockout easy to make?

Purple Cow

Ingredients:

1 cup grape juice
½ pint vanilla ice cream
1 tablespoon sugar
lemon-lime soda

Utensils:

blender
ice cream scoop
measuring cup
measuring spoon
2 glasses
2 straws

Directions:

1. Put the grape juice, the ice cream, and the sugar into the blender.

2. Blend at medium speed for 15 seconds.

3. Pour even amounts of the mixture into the 2 glasses.

4. Finish filling the glasses by pouring lemon-lime soda into them.

5. Place a straw in each glass and serve. What a treat!

Purple Cow

Vocabulary:

Nouns	*Verbs*	*Modifiers*
amounts	blend	even or equal
blender	fill	lemon-lime
grape juice	finish	medium
ice cream scoop	place	vanilla
measuring cup	pour	
measuring spoon	put	
mixture	serve	
pint		
seconds		
soda		
speed		
straws		
tablespoon		

Activities:

Have the children describe the ingredients by appearance, texture, temperature, and taste. Ask the children how the ingredients are alike, and how they are different.

Have the children describe what they think the end product will look like before you mix anything together.

Substitute a different kind of juice, and have the children compare the two drinks. Ask them which kind they prefer.

Use different amounts of ice cream for separate batches. Have the children compare the taste and appearance of each recipe.

Zesty Extras:

Purple Cow

Blooming Questions:

Knowledge

What animal is named in the recipe? *cow*
Name the ingredients we used to make a Purple Cow.
  grape juice, vanilla ice cream, sugar, lemon-lime soda
How did we get the ice cream out of its container? *with an ice cream scoop*
How many glasses did this recipe make? *two*

Comprehension

Tell how to make this drink. *See the recipe.*
Describe how a Purple Cow tastes. *a sweet, cold drink made with ice cream and grape juice*
When we added the soda, did the drink get frozen or foamy? *foamy*
Where should we keep the leftover grape juice? *in the refrigerator or freezer*

Application

Name something that's similar to an ice cream scoop. *a spoon, a ladle*
Why did we use a blender to mix the ingredients?
  to make sure all the ingredients were mixed well without spilling them
What other foods could we put in a blender? *bananas, strawberries, eggs, onions, nuts, etc.*
Show how to use a blender safely. *Answers will vary.*

Analysis

What flavor is a Purple Cow? *grape*
How are grape juice and lemon-lime soda alike? *both are drinks*
How are they different?
  *grape juice is purple, but lemon-lime soda is yellow/green; have different flavors; soda is
  carbonated*
What would happen if we left the ice cream out of the recipe?
  The drink wouldn't be as thick, and the flavor would be different.
Where does grape juice come from? *grapes*

Synthesis

What ingredients could we add to this recipe? *Answers will vary.*
What could we use instead of lemon-lime soda? *other kinds of soda*
What could we do if we didn't have a blender? *Mix it by hand.*
Suppose you're having a purple party and serving only purple foods. What could you serve
  besides Purple Cows? *Answers will vary.*

Evaluation

Compare a Purple Cow to your favorite drink.
Is *Purple Cow* a good name for this drink?
Think of a different name for this recipe.
How did you think of this new name?

Banana Blitz

Ingredients:

1 large ripe banana
ice cubes
¼ cup cold water
¼ cup instant powdered milk
¼ teaspoon vanilla
1 teaspoon honey

Utensils:

blender
glass
hammer
measuring cup
measuring spoons
paring knife
plastic bag

Directions:

1. Peel the banana.

2. Cut the banana into four pieces.

3. Place ice cubes in the plastic bag. Pound the ice cubes with the hammer until you have ¼ cup of crushed ice.

4. Put all of the ingredients into the blender.

5. Blend at medium speed for one minute.

6. Pour into the glass and serve.

Banana Blitz

Vocabulary:

Nouns	*Verbs*	*Modifiers*
blender	blend	crushed
half	cut	instant
hammer	place	large
honey	pound	medium
measuring cup	pour	powdered
measuring spoons	put	ripe
paring knife	serve	sharp
plastic bag	slice	
speed		
teaspoon		
vanilla		

Activities:

Discuss the concepts of *half* and *quarter* as you cut the banana. Have the children practice cutting bananas different ways.

Have the children take turns pounding the ice. Have them predict how many ice cubes it will take to equal ¼ cup of crushed ice.

Have the children measure an ice cube in a measuring cup before and after crushing. Ask the children to compare the two measurements.

Discuss the purpose of a blender. Ask the children what it does, what kinds of foods you could blend, and the texture of foods before and after blending.

Zesty Extras:

15

Banana Blitz

Blooming Questions:

Knowledge

Which utensils did we use for measuring? *measuring cups, measuring spoons*
What did we do with the banana? *peeled it, cut it into four pieces*
What kind of milk did we use? *instant powdered milk*
What did we serve the drink in? *a glass*

Comprehension

Describe what a banana looks like.
   yellow outside, white inside; thick peel; brown spots; has tiny seeds
How many pieces did we cut the banana into? *four*
Why did we need a hammer? *to crush the ice*
Does *ripe* mean *ready to eat* or *not ready to eat*? *ready to eat*

Application

What do we usually pound with a hammer? *nails*
What else could we make with bananas? *banana splits, banana cream pie, banana bread, etc.*
What kind of food is a banana? *fruit*
Name all the fruit drinks you can think of.
   lemonade, grape juice, apple cider, pineapple juice, orange juice, etc.

Analysis

Which ingredient makes this drink sweet, sugar or milk? *sugar*
Finish this sentence: Ice is frozen _____. *water*
Why did we cut the banana? *to make it easier to blend*
How many bananas would it take to make eight Banana Blitzes? *eight*

Synthesis

Name something we could use to crush the ice if we didn't have a hammer.
   a brick, a heavy rock, a rolling pin, a meat tenderizer, etc.
What would happen if we didn't crush the ice?
   The blender would have to work very hard and the drink might have lumps of ice.
How can we change this recipe if nobody likes bananas? *Substitute a different fruit.*
What would be another fancy name for this drink? *Answers will vary.*

Evaluation

Is there something better we could have used to crush the ice in?
Is a Banana Blitz junk food?
Is a Banana Blitz expensive to make?
How would you decide whether to make lemonade or a Banana Blitz for some thirsty friends?

Ice Cream Float

Ingredients:

ice cream
soda pop

Utensils:

glass
ice cream scoop
spoon
straw

Directions:

1. Put one scoop of ice cream into the glass.

2. Pour soda pop into glass slowly so that the foam will not spill over the sides of the glass. Keep adding soda until the foam reaches the top of the glass.

3. Serve with a spoon and a drinking straw.

Ice Cream Float

Vocabulary:

Nouns	Verbs	Modifier
foam	pour	cool
ice cream	spill	
ice cream scoop		
soda pop		
spoon		
straw		

Activities:

Let the children get a scoopful of ice cream and a spoonful of ice cream. Have them compare the size of the ice cream after it is removed from the carton with either the scoop or the spoon. Explain that ice cream is a dairy product (made from milk, etc.).

Discuss with the children why it is important to pour the soda slowly into the glass. Have one child demonstrate what can happen if the soda is poured in too quickly. Talk about carbonation, comparing a glass of water to a glass of soda pop.

Have the children discuss why a spoon is needed in addition to a drinking straw when serving this drink.

Zesty Extras:

Ice Cream Float

Blooming Questions:

Knowledge

What is the name of this recipe? *Ice Cream Float*
What did we add to the ice cream? *soda pop*
What happened when we added the soda pop? *it foamed, made an ice cream float*
What flavor of ice cream did we use? *Answers will vary.*

Comprehension

Which of these things are ingredients for an ice cream float? soda pop, syrup, ice cream,
  cookie, candy, jelly *soda pop, ice cream*
Is a drink made with ice cream and soda pop a milk shake or a float? *float*
Listen. Ice cream grows on trees. Is that true? *No*
Describe how to make an ice cream float. *See the recipe.*

Application

What other drinks are made with ice cream? *milk shake, malt*
You need a spoon and a straw to eat an ice cream float. What is another drink you eat with a
  spoon and straw? *root beer float, ice cream soda, malt, shake*
Why will soda pop spill over the top of the glass if you pour it too quickly?
  The faster you pour soda pop, the more it foams.

Analysis

Which do we add first, the ice cream or the soda pop? *ice cream*
How are the containers for pop and ice cream the same? *both are containers*
How are they different? *pop bottle is glass or plastic, ice cream carton is cardboard*
What is ice cream made of? *milk or cream, sugar, and flavoring*

Synthesis

Draw a new kind of glass that every child would want to use to make an ice cream float.
  Answers will vary.
Invent your own ice cream flavor for an ice cream float. Tell about your creation.
  Answers will vary.
Now, think of a new name for an ice cream float made with the ice cream flavor you created.
  What would you call it? *Answers will vary.*

Evaluation

What are some good and bad things about an ice cream float?
Would an ice cream float be a good drink for a hot day?
What's your favorite kind of ice cream float?
Tell why a dentist may not approve of this expression, "An ice cream float a day keeps the
  dentist away."

Eggstra Special Delight

Ingredients:

1 egg
1 cup cold milk
1 tablespoon honey
¼ teaspoon vanilla
ground nutmeg

Utensils:

cup
hand or electric mixer
measuring cup
measuring spoons
mixing bowl

Directions:

1. Break the egg into the bowl.

2. Beat the egg with the mixer for 1 minute (low speed for electric mixer).

3. Add the milk, honey, and vanilla to the beaten egg.

4. Beat all the ingredients about 1 minute (medium speed for electric mixer) until the mixture looks frothy.

5. Pour the mixture into a cup.

6. Sprinkle a little nutmeg on top of the eggnog.

7. Serve and enjoy!

Eggstra Special Delight

Vocabulary:

Nouns	*Verbs*	*Modifiers*
electric mixer	break (an egg)	beaten (egg)
honey	sprinkle	frothy
liquid		white
measuring cup		
measuring spoons		
mixing bowl		
nutmeg		
shell		
vanilla		
yolk		

Activities:

Explain that Eggstra Special Delight is a fancy name for eggnog.

Talk about holidays when eggnog is popular, such as Christmas or New Year's.

Let the children discuss what happens to the egg while it is being beaten. Do the same thing when all the ingredients are beaten together.

Bring whole nutmeg for the children to observe. Grate the nutmeg with a fine grater. Let the children compare the smell and taste of freshly grated nutmeg and ground nutmeg from a spice can or jar.

Since Eggstra Special Delight is often served heated, heat a portion of this recipe and let the children compare the taste at the two temperatures.

Zesty Extras:

Eggstra Special Delight

Blooming Questions:

Knowledge

What is the hard part of a raw egg called? *shell*
What do we call the yellow part inside the egg? *yolk*
What do we call the white part inside the egg? *white*

Comprehension

What animal lays the eggs we used to make Eggstra Special Delight? *chicken*
Where does honey come from? *bees*
What does the word *frothy* mean? *foamy, filled with tiny bubbles*
We used milk, egg, and honey to make this recipe. What else did we use? *vanilla, nutmeg*

Application

Finish this sentence: Bees make _____. *honey*
How are vanilla and nutmeg alike? *both flavorings*
How are they different? *vanilla is liquid, nutmeg is solid*
Eggstra Special Delight is a drink made of milk and other things. What other drinks are made of milk? *cocoa, milk shake, malt*

Analysis

Tell me all the parts of an egg. *shell, yolk, egg white*
Which part don't we eat? *shell*
Tell the steps we followed to make Eggstra Special Delight. *See the recipe.*
Which ingredient makes this drink sweet? *honey*

Synthesis

Eggstra Special Delight is a holiday drink. Create another special drink for your favorite holiday. *Answers will vary.*
What other seasonings or spices could we add to this recipe? *cinnamon, cloves, chocolate*
How would you change the color of Eggstra Special Delight? *use food coloring*

Evaluation

Taste some Eggstra Special Delight with and without nutmeg. Which way do you like better?
Which would you rather drink on a hot summer day, Eggstra Special Delight or lemonade?
What foods would you like to eat with Eggstra Special Delight?
Is Eggstra Special Delight a healthy drink?

Pear-fection

Ingredients:

canned pear halves, chilled
cheddar cheese, grated
maraschino cherries
mayonnaise

Utensils:

can opener
grater
plate
small spoon

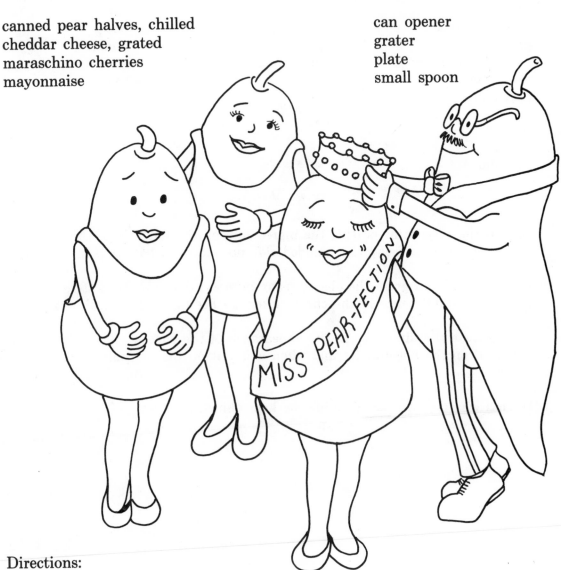

Directions:

1. Open the can of pears. Drain the juice out of the can.

2. Place pear halves on a plate with the flat side of each pear half facing up.

3. Put a spoonful of mayonnaise on the middle of each pear half.

4. Sprinkle some grated cheese on top of the mayonnaise.

5. Put a cherry on top of the grated cheese.

6. Serve with pride!

Pear-fection

Vocabulary:

Nouns	Verbs	Modifiers
can opener	drain	chilled
cheddar cheese	grate	flat
grater	open	middle
maraschino cherry	put	small
mayonnaise	sprinkle	top
pear half		
plate		
salad		
spoon		
spoonful		

Activities: Discuss the reason for putting the ingredients on the flat side of the pear. Make a pear salad using the rounded side up and see what happens.

Have the children grate the cheese using different sides of the grater. Compare the difference in the cheese after it's been grated on each side.

Demonstrate the difference in the appearance of the cheese when it is sprinkled on the mayonnaise and when it is put on the mayonnaise with a spoon.

Discuss why the pear salad should be kept chilled.

Zesty Extras:

Pear-fection

Blooming Questions:

Knowledge

What ingredients do we need to make a Pear-fection? *pears, cheese, cherries, mayonnaise*
Where do we put the mayonnaise? *in the hole on the flat side of the pear*
Do we slice the cheese or grate it? *grate it*

Comprehension

Tell how we made the Pear-fection. *See the recipe.*
Why do we keep the pears cold? *to keep them fresh, so they taste better*
Finish this sentence: A pear and a cherry are both _____. *fruit, food*

Application

We keep leftover Pear-fection in the refrigerator. What else do we keep there?
  milk, eggs, meats, vegetables
What else can you make with pears? *dessert, Jell-O, jelly, juice*
What would happen if we didn't drain the pears? *The salad would be too watery.*

Analysis

What is cheese made from? *milk*
Where do pears grow? *on pear trees*
What parts of a pear are removed before they are canned? *core, stem, and skin*
Is there more cheese or fruit in Pear-fection? *fruit*

Synthesis

What would happen if we used a whole pear without slicing it?
  We'd have no place to put the mayonnaise.
What other ingredients could we add to this recipe? *lettuce, nuts*
What other fruits could we use instead of the pear? *peaches, pineapple, apple*
How would that change the recipe? *would taste different, name would change*

Evaluation

What did you like best about this salad?
What did you like least?
Do you think this is a pretty dish? What makes it pretty?
Which do you prefer, tossed salad or Pear-fection?

25

Apple-Raisin Jumble

Ingredients:

2 apples
½ cup raisins
½ cups pecans, chopped
mayonnaise

Utensils:

large mixing spoon
measuring cup
mixing bowl
paring knife
small spoon

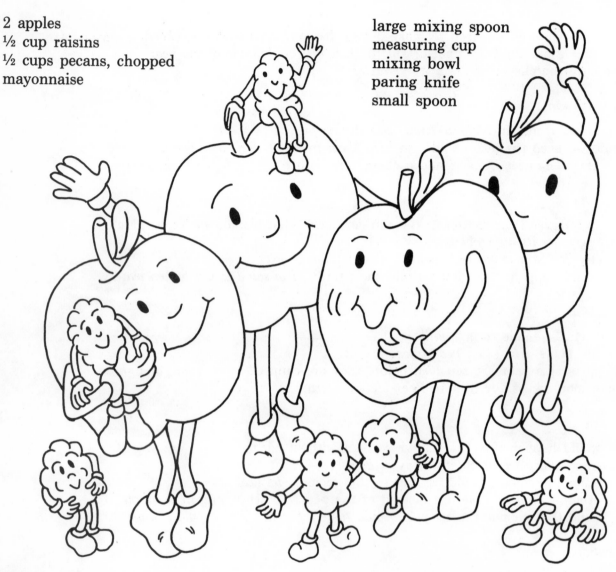

Directions:

1. Cut the apples into quarters. Remove the core from each quarter.

2. Cut the apple pieces into bite-sized pieces. Put the pieces into the mixing bowl.

3. Add the raisins and pecans to the apple pieces.

4. Add a few spoonfuls of mayonnaise to the above ingredients. Stir until all ingredients are coated with mayonnaise.

5. Serve with a smile!

Apple-Raisin Jumble

Vocabulary:

Nouns	Verbs	Modifiers
apple	add	all
core	cut	bite-sized
mayonnaise	put	chopped
measuring cup	remove	coated
paring knife	stir	each
pecan		few
quarters		
raisin		
salad		
spoonful		

Activities:

Discuss the terms *half*, *quarter*, and *whole* as you cut each apple into quarters.

Show the children the core of the apple and discuss what is contained in the core. Discuss why the core is not edible.

Ask the children what would happen to the seeds if they were planted. If possible, show pictures of actual seeds growing and an apple tree.

Ask the children to describe bite-sized pieces.

Zesty Extras:

Apple-Raisin Jumble

Blooming Questions:

Knowledge

What is the name of this recipe? *Apple-Raisin Jumble*
What did we use to measure the raisins and pecans? *measuring cup*
What is inside the core of an apple? *seeds*

Comprehension

What ingredients do we need to make this recipe? *apples, raisins, pecans, and mayonnaise*
Describe what we did to the apples. *See the recipe.*
How big is a bite-sized piece? *about the size you could easily chew*
Where do apples come from? *apple trees*

Application

What would happen if we peeled the apple first? *The mixture would not be as colorful.*
How would it taste if we left out the mayonnaise? *drier, less tangy*
Apple-Raisin Jumble has nuts in it. What other foods have nuts? *brownies, cookies, cereals*

Analysis

What makes Apple-Raisin Jumble crunchy? *pecans and apples*
What makes it sweet? *apples and raisins*
How does each ingredient taste?
   apples and raisins taste sweet, pecans are crunchy, mayonnaise is tangy
How many quarters are in one apple? *four*

Synthesis

What other ingredients could you use to make the Apple-Raisin Jumble crunchy?
   lettuce, other nuts, celery
What could you add to make it sweeter? *sugar or honey*
What could you use instead of the mayonnaise? *whipped cream, ice cream*
Let's pretend we're serving this recipe for dessert. What could we change to make it special?
   Answers may vary.

Evaluation

What is your favorite way to eat apples?
Do you like raisins?
What ingredient do you think tastes best?
What's the best kind of apple to use in this recipe?

Salad of the Sea

Ingredients:

1 small can tuna
2 teaspoons sweet pickle relish
1 teaspoon chopped onion
1 hard-boiled egg
mayonnaise
lettuce

Utensils:

can opener
large mixing spoon
measuring spoons
mixing bowl
paring knife
small spoon

Directions:

1. Open the can of tuna and drain the liquid from the can. Place the drained tuna in a mixing bowl.

2. Put the relish and the onion into the bowl with the tuna.

3. Peel the boiled egg. Chop the egg into small pieces and put them into the bowl with the other ingredients.

4. Put a few spoonfuls of mayonnaise into the bowl and mix well with the other ingredients.

5. Serve the tuna salad on a lettuce leaf.

Salad of the Sea

Vocabulary:

Nouns	Verbs	Modifiers
can opener	chop	chopped
egg	drain	few
lettuce leaf	mix well	hard-boiled
liquid	open	small
mayonnaise	peel	
onion	place	
salad	put	
sweet pickle relish		
teaspoon		
tuna		

Activities:

Discuss why the liquid should be drained and what would happen to the tuna salad if the liquid remained with the tuna.

Talk about how to chop the onion and let the children chop it themselves. Discuss what happens to the onion and what happens to them as they chop the onion.

Discuss the process of peeling the egg and chopping it into pieces. Compare the appearance of a hard-boiled egg and an uncooked one, both inside and out.

Zesty Extras:

30

Salad of the Sea

Blooming Questions:

Knowledge

What is the name of this recipe? *Salad of the Sea*
What ingredients did we use? *tuna, pickle relish, egg, mayonnaise, onion, lettuce*
Did we use a whole onion? *no*
What kind of eggs did we use? *hard-boiled*

Comprehension

Describe how to fix the onion. *See the recipe.*
What happened to our eyes when we chopped the onion? *Our eyes watered.*
What happened to our eyes when we chopped the egg? *nothing*
Why did we drain the liquid from the tuna? *so the salad wouldn't be watery*

Application

What other foods do you chop before you add them to recipes?
  ham, carrots, potatoes, strawberries, etc.
What other foods must you drain before eating? *spaghetti, macaroni, canned fruits, vegetables*
Why did we peel the egg before we chopped it? *so we didn't have any eggshell in the salad*

Analysis

What are the parts of an egg? *shell, white, yolk*
Do a hard-boiled and a raw egg have the same parts? *yes*
How are they different? *hard-boiled egg — hard, solid, cooked; raw egg — soft, liquid, uncooked*

Synthesis

What could be another name for this recipe? Why? *Answers will vary.*
What could you leave out of this recipe? *relish, onion, or egg*
How would it change the taste? *Answers will vary.*
Could you still call it *Salad of the Sea*? *yes*

Evaluation

What was the easiest part of this recipe?
What was hardest part?
Which way is your favorite way to serve tuna salad?
Would you rather have tuna salad for breakfast or for lunch?

Sweet'n'Sticky Sandwich

Ingredients:

2 slices of bread
peanut butter
jelly

Utensils:

table knife

Directions:

1. Spread some peanut butter on one slice of bread.

2. Spread some jelly on the other bread slice.

3. Put the two pieces of bread together so that the peanut butter and jelly touch each other.

4. Slice the sandwich in half.

5. Serve.

Sweet 'n' Sticky Sandwich

Vocabulary:

Nouns	*Verbs*	*Modifiers*
bread	put	other
jelly	spread	small
knife	touch	some
peanut butter		together
sandwich		
slice		

Activities:

Discuss why the peanut butter and jelly should only be spread on one side of the bread. Talk about what would happen if both sides were covered with peanut butter and jelly.

Ask the children to explain why the sandwich is put together so that the peanut butter and jelly touch each other.

Cut the sandwiches in half in different directions (horizontal, vertical, diagonal). Ask the children to compare the halves to see whether they are larger or smaller, depending on the cutting pattern.

Zesty Extras:

Sweet 'n' Sticky Sandwich

Blooming Questions:

Knowledge

What is the name of this recipe? *Sweet 'n' Sticky Sandwich*
What ingredients do we need to make it? *bread, peanut butter, jelly*
How many slices of bread do we need for one sandwich? *two*

Comprehension

What's another name for this sandwich? *peanut butter and jelly sandwich*
How did we put the peanut butter and jelly on the bread? *spread it with a knife*
Tell the steps to making a peanut butter and jelly sandwich. *See the recipe.*

Application

What would happen if we used a sharp knife?
  It wouldn't spread as smoothly, and we might cut ourselves.
What other utensils could we use to spread the ingredients? *spatula, spoon*
What other foods do we spread on bread? *cheese spread, cream cheese, mustard, mayonnaise*
Name another food that's like jelly. *jam, preserves*

Analysis

What is peanut butter made of? *peanuts*
What is jelly made of? *fruits and sugar*
How many slices of bread would we need to make three sandwiches? *six*
Which has more protein, peanut butter or bread? *peanut butter*

Synthesis

What other ingredients could we add to the recipe to make it different? *bananas, raisins, etc.*
How would each one change the taste? *Answers will vary.*
Name two different kinds of bread we could use in this recipe. *Answers will vary.*
Draw a creative shape for a peanut butter and jelly sandwich. *Answers will vary.*

Evaluation

What kind of jelly is your favorite?
Do you like chunky or creamy peanut butter better?
Are all brands of peanut butter alike?
Is this a good sandwich for young children to make?

All-American Sandwich

Ingredients:

1 slice of ham
1 slice of American Cheese
1 leaf of lettuce
dab of mustard
dab of mayonnaise
2 slices of bread

Utensils:

table knife with a blunt edge
table knife with a serrated edge

Directions:

1. Spread a dab of mayonnaise on one slice of bread.

2. Put the lettuce leaf on top of the mayonnaise.

3. Place the ham slice on top of the lettuce.

4. Place the cheese slice on top of the ham slice.

5. Spread a dab of mustard on the remaining slice of bread.

6. Place this slice of bread on top of the cheese slice so that the mustard touches the cheese.

7. Cut the sandwich in half.

8. Serve and enjoy!

All-American Sandwich

Vocabulary:

Nouns	*Verbs*	*Modifiers*
bread	cut	blunt
cheese	serve	remaining
dab	spread	serrated
edge		wheat
half		
ham		
lettuce		
mayonnaise		
mustard		
slice		

Activities:

As the children spread the mustard and mayonnaise on the bread, discuss why only one side of the bread is coated. What would happen if both sides were coated?

Rearrange the sequence of making the sandwich (e.g., using the mustard first, then the cheese slice, then the lettuce, and then the ham slice). Discuss whether or not the change in sequence makes a difference in the outcome.

Show the children the difference between a table knife with a serrated edge and a table knife with a blunt edge. Talk about why a knife with a serrated edge makes it easier to cut the sandwich in half.

Talk about the differences between wheat bread and white bread. Wheat bread is darker than white bread. Nutritionists say that wheat bread is healthier because wheat is a natural grain.

Zesty Extras:

All-American Sandwich

Blooming Questions:

Knowledge

Show me the knife with the serrated edge. *points to serrated knife*
How much lettuce did we use? *one leaf*
Which one is meat, cheese or ham? *ham*

Comprehension

What did we do with the serrated knife? *sliced the sandwich*
Is sliced ham flat? *yes*
What else did we put on our sandwich that is flat? *cheese*
We spread mayonnaise on one slice of bread. What did we spread on the other slice? *mustard*
How can we tell the difference between mayonnaise and mustard?
   mayonnaise is white, mustard is yellow; mustard is spicier than mayonnaise

Application

The cheese we used is American cheese. What other kinds of cheese have you eaten?
   Answers will vary.
Lettuce is good on sandwiches. What other recipes do we use lettuce in? *salads*
If we didn't have two slices of bread, how could we make a sandwich that still had top and
   bottom bread slices? *Cut one slice in half.*

Analysis

Why did we use the serrated knife for cutting the sandwich? *easier to cut without tearing bread*
Describe mayonnaise. *white, creamy, tangy, spreads easily*
What do you think mayonnaise is made from? *egg yolks and lemon or vinegar*
Now, describe mustard. *yellow, smooth, spicy*
What is mustard made from? *mustard seeds, vinegar, salt*

Synthesis

Let's invent a new sandwich. What ingredients should we use? *Answers will vary.*
Some people use other food instead of bread slices to make a sandwich. Can you think of one?
   rolls, buns
Mayonnaise and mustard are two things we used to make our sandwich spicy. What other
   spicy things do people put on sandwiches? *pepper, onions, chili peppers, horseradish, etc.*

Evaluation

Do you like the taste of mustard?
If we hadn't cut the sandwich in half, would it still be a sandwich?
Which do you like better, this ham and cheese sandwich or a peanut butter and jelly sandwich?

Tomato Party Rounds

Ingredients:

whole wheat bread
softened butter
cherry tomatoes
large sprig of fresh dill
mayonnaise

Utensils:

table knife
paring knife
rolling pin
round cookie cutter
small spoon

Directions:

1. Flatten the bread slices slightly with the rolling pin.

2. Spread the butter thinly on flattened bread with the table knife.

3. Using the cookie cutter, cut rounds of bread.

4. Slice the tomatoes thinly with the paring knife.

5. Put a tomato slice on top of each round of bread.

6. Using the spoon, place a small dab of mayonnaise on top of each tomato slice.

7. Garnish the top of each round with a spring of fresh dill.

8. Now, let's have a party!

Tomato Party Rounds

Vocabulary:

Nouns	*Verbs*	*Modifiers*
bread	cut	fresh
butter	flatten	on top
cookie cutter	garnish	slightly
dab	slice	small
dill	spread	thinly
mayonnaise	taste	
rolling pin		
rounds		
sprig		
tomatoes		

Activities:

Show the children whole wheat and white bread and let them discuss the difference in taste, texture, and appearance.

Show the children the cherry tomatoes and regular tomato. See if they can tell why the small tomato is called a "cherry" tomato.

Before flattening the bread slice, help the children imagine what will happen to the bread's appearance after it is rolled. Let them decide if the taste will be different, too.

If possible, have the children use different sizes of cookie cutters. Talk about the differences among the shapes and sizes of the various cut-outs.

Zesty Extras:

Tomato Party Rounds

Blooming Questions:

Knowledge

What are two utensils we used to make Tomato Party Rounds? *See the utensils list.*
I'm thinking of something small, round, and red. What am I thinking of? *cherry tomato*
We used two things that we spread. What are they? *butter and mayonnaise*
Is our cookie cutter round or square? *round*

Comprehension

Describe the dill we used. How does it look, smell, and taste? *Answers will vary.*
Why did we slice the tomatoes? *so they would stay flat on the bread*
Listen. Mayonnaise and mustard are soft. Is that true? *yes*
Listen again. I made a cherry pie with cherry tomatoes. Does that sound right? *no*

Application

We used mayonnaise on these Party Rounds. What other recipes use mayonnaise?
  tuna salad, deviled eggs, etc.
The bread we used feels soft. What other word can you think of that means almost the same
  thing as "soft"? *squishy*
Tomatoes are red vegetables. What other red vegetables can you think of?
  beets, red cabbage, radishes
We cut out the bread rounds with the rolling pin. Does that sound right?
  Explain your answer. *no — We cut them with a cookie cutter.*

Analysis

We made these Party Rounds out of bread, tomatoes, and dill. What else did we use?
  mayonnaise and butter
Let's look at a slice of tomato. What parts does it have? *seeds, pulp, skin, juice*
I don't like tomatoes. Tell me how I could make a Party Round without using a tomato.
  Answers will vary.

Synthesis

Tomatoes are used in many recipes. Name some of your favorite foods that have tomatoes in
  them. *Answers will vary.*
How are a cherry tomato and a regular tomato alike? *both tomatoes*
How are they different? *cherry tomatoes are smaller*
Do they taste the same? *yes*
A sharp knife is one that cuts well. What do I mean when I say, "You children have sharp
  minds"? *You are good thinkers.*

Evaluation

Do you like the taste of these Party Rounds?
Would you like the taste of dill if you ate it by itself?
Butter is a dairy product. How do I know that?
Why do you think this recipe name has the word *party* in it?

Bumps on a Log

Ingredients:

8 celery stalks
peanut butter
raisins

Utensils:

paper towels
paring knife
plate
table knife
vegetable brush

Directions:

1. Wash the celery with the vegetable brush.

2. Cut off the leaves and trim ¼ inch off the top and bottom of each stalk.

3. Dry each stalk with a paper towel.

4. Cut each stalk into 3 equal pieces.

5. Spread peanut butter on each piece of celery. These are your "logs"!

6. Put 3 or 4 raisins on each "log." Now you have "Bumps on a Log!"

7. Arrange the logs on the plate and serve.

Bumps on a Log

Vocabulary:

Nouns	*Verbs*	*Modifiers*
bump	spread	crunchy
celery stalk	trim	equal
log		
peanut butter		
raisin		
vegetable brush		

Activities:

Show the children that dirt is on the inside and the outside of a celery stalk. Demonstrate that the vegetable brush is stiff enough to remove the dirt. Let the children wash the celery.

Let the children dry the clean stalks. Have them experiment with putting peanut butter on wet celery and on dry celery. Ask them which way worked better.

Let the children smell and taste the celery. Talk about how "crunchy" the celery is when the children chew it. Explain that celery is a vegetable that can be eaten raw or cooked. It can be used in salads or soups, or just eaten plain.

Tell the children how each of the ingredients is made. Let them taste each ingredient separately. Explain why each individual ingredient is good for them and why this recipe makes a nutritious snack.

Zesty Extras:

Bumps on a Log

Blooming Questions:

Knowledge

What kind of food is celery? *vegetable*
Which ingredient did we spread with a knife? *peanut butter*
Show me the knife that is better for cutting. *paring knife*
Now, show me the knife that is better for spreading. *table knife*

Comprehension

Listen. Peanut butter is a dairy product. Is that true? *no*
Finish this sentence: Celery and lettuce are both _____. *vegetables*
Tell how we made Bumps on a Log. *See the recipe.*
What does "crunchy" mean? *crisp; makes noise when you chew it*

Application

Peanut butter comes in a jar. What other foods come in a jar?
   jelly, pickles, mustard, mayonnaise, catsup, etc.
What kinds of knives can you think of? *sharp, paring, butcher, bread, table, butter*
What other foods are crunchy when you chew them? *carrots, potato chips, etc.*

Analysis

Tell me an ingredient of Bumps on a Log that isn't a vegetable. *peanut butter or raisins*
Tell me an ingredient that's made from grapes. *raisins*
Tell me two ingredients you can't spread. *celery, raisins*
If we cut a celery stalk in half, will the pieces be equal? *yes*

Synthesis

How is a vegetable brush like a toothbrush? *both have bristles, both for cleaning*
If we didn't have raisins, what could we use for the "bumps" in this recipe? *Answers will vary.*
Pretend you'd like to make up a new dessert called "Turtles on a Log." What ingredients
   could you use? *Answers will vary.*

Evaluation

What's the most fun part of making Bumps on a Log?
Which filling do you like better, peanut butter or cream cheese?
If you could eat peanut butter on anything, not just celery, what would you choose?
Would Bumps on a Log make a good party snack?

Toothpick Kabobs

Ingredients:

melon balls
pineapple chunks
cold meat chunks
cubes of cheese
small wieners
olives
pickle cubes
orange slices
banana slices
bread cubes

Utensils:

party toothpicks

Directions:

1. Select two or three of the above ingredients.

2. Choose a toothpick.

3. Push the toothpick through each of the ingredients until the toothpick is full.

4. Repeat the steps until all of the toothpicks or ingredients have been used.

5. Arrange on a plate and serve.

Toothpick Kabobs

Vocabulary:

Nouns	Verbs	Modifiers
Nouns	*Verbs*	*Modifiers*
balls	arrange	full
banana	choose	party
cheese	push	small
chunks	repeat	
cubes	select	
kabobs	serve	
melon	use	
olives		
orange		
pickle		
pineapple		
toothpicks		
wieners		

Activities:

Let several children make their own kabobs at the same time. Then, have them compare how each of their kabobs is different or the same from the others. How do they look different? How do they feel different? How do they taste different?

Discuss with the children what combinations of food might taste the worst, or the best. Why do certain foods taste good together, such as a pineapple chunk and a banana slice? Why do other foods taste bad together, such as a pickle cube and an orange slice?

Talk with the children about how easy or how hard it is to push a toothpick into certain foods. Have them feel how a toothpick goes into an olive, a bread cube, a cube of cheese, and a melon ball.

Help the children guess how many ingredients can fit onto a toothpick. Discuss why more ingredients can sometimes fit on a toothpick than other times. How could they make more ingredients fit on the toothpick?

Place different combinations on the toothpicks and compare the weights of the kabobs. Why do two wieners and a melon ball weigh more than a kabob with just two wieners? Why do three bread cubes on a kabob weigh less than two orange slices?

Zesty Extras:

Toothpick Kabobs

Blooming Questions:

Knowledge

What did we use to hold the pieces of food together? *toothpicks*
Name the different kinds of food we put on the toothpicks. *See the recipe.*
What were the juiciest foods we used? *pineapple, melon, orange slices*

Comprehension

Tell how we made our Toothpick Kabobs. *See the recipe.*
Now, show me how we made the kabobs without talking to me. *pantomimes appropriately*
Describe a Toothpick Kabob. *pieces or cubes of different foods on a toothpick*

Application

Name all the fruits we could use to make a kabob. *Answers will vary.*
Name all the meats we could use. *Answers will vary.*
What foods must be cooked before we use them for kabobs? *bread, meats*

Analysis

What are toothpicks made of? *wood or plastic*
How many cubes of cheese would fit on one toothpick?
  Answers will vary depending on the cube size.
Why is it important to use small pieces of food?
  so we can fit several pieces on each toothpick
Why didn't we cut up the olives into smaller pieces?
  They are already small enough.
Why did we use only one toothpick for each kabob? *One is all we need.*

Synthesis

What could we put on the toothpicks to make our kabobs sweeter? *sugar or honey*
What kinds of cheese could we use if we just wanted cheese kabobs?
  cheddar, Swiss, colby, etc.
What foods could we use to make special Valentine's Day kabobs? *Answers will vary.*

Evaluation

When would be the best time to serve our Toothpick Kabobs?
What kind of food would be the easiest to slice or cube?
What kind of food would be the most difficult?
Why wouldn't you want to have a Toothpick Kabob for your main food at a meal?

46

Triple-Treat Sandwich Loaf

Ingredients:

1 loaf of whole-wheat bread, unsliced
chicken salad spread*
ham salad spread*
egg salad spread*

Utensils:

large serrated knife
small spreading knife

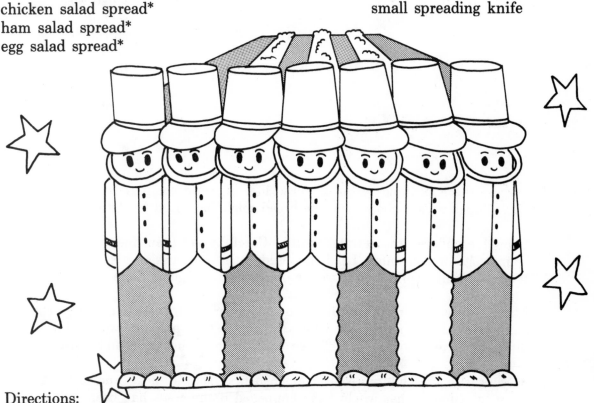

Directions:

1. Cut the loaf of bread lengthwise into four equal layers.

2. Spread the chicken salad on the top side of the bottom layer.

3. Place the next layer of bread on top of the chicken salad.

4. Spread the ham salad on top of the second layer of bread.

5. Place the next layer of bread on top of the ham salad.

6. Spread the egg salad on top of the third layer of bread.

7. Place the final layer of bread on top of the egg salad.

8. Cut crosswise slices through all layers of the sandwich loaf. **Arrange the slices on a plate and serve.**

* Any preferred filling may be substituted.

Triple-Treat Sandwich Loaf

Vocabulary:

Nouns	*Verbs*	*Modifiers*
bread	arrange	bottom
chicken salad	cut	crosswise
egg salad	place	lengthwise
ham salad	serve	second
knife	spread	serrated
layer		third
loaf		top
sandwich		unsliced
side		whole wheat
spread		

Activities:

Discuss the appearance of an unsliced loaf of bread compared to a loaf of sliced bread. Talk about how the bread might be sliced in the bakery.

Show the children the serrated knife. Carefully, let them feel the uneven, sharp edge of the knife. Lead the children in a discussion about why this type of a knife works better to cut bread than a regular knife does.

Many different fillings could be used in the sandwich loaf. Encourage the children to think of different fillings to use. Then, prepare two or three different loaves and let the children compare how they look and taste.

Discuss with the children what happened first, second, next, and last. Ask them to tell you what would have happened if the steps had been switched, or if the same step had been done twice.

Zesty Extras:

Triple-Treat Sandwich Loaf

Blooming Questions:

Knowledge

What three kinds of salad spread did we use? *chicken salad, ham salad, and egg salad*
Whch knife did we use to slice the bread? *child points to serrated knife*
What did we do with the small knife? *spread the fillings*
What kind of bread did we use? *whole wheat*

Comprehension

Tell how we made Triple-Treat Sandwich Loaf. *See the recipe.*
What is chicken salad (ham salad, egg salad) made from? *Accept appropriate answers.*
Why should we put the top piece of bread on our sandwich loaf?
  to keep the filling in place

Application

What other kinds of spreads could we use for our sandwich loaf?
  cheese spread, liverwurst, cream cheese
What other kinds of bread could we use? *white, rye, oatmeal, potato*
A sandwich loaf is one kind of layer food. What other kinds of layer food could we make?
  parfait, cake, hamburger, sandwich

Analysis

Why did we cut the bread into four layers? *so we could spread on the three different fillings*
Does it matter which spread we put on first? *no*
Why didn't we use the large serrated knife for spreading?
  It wouldn't spread as smoothly as the smaller, flat knife.
Did we use more layers of bread or filling? *bread*

Synthesis

How could we make a triple-treat dessert loaf? *Answers will vary.*
How could we make our sandwich loaf taste even better? *Answers will vary.*
Why do we call this a Triple-Treat Sandwich Loaf?
  There are three fillings in this sandwich instead of one.
What would happen if we just sliced the bread in half and spread all the salad spreads
  together? *It would be too fat to eat.*

Evaluation

Would you eat Triple-Treat Sandwich Loaf if we frosted it with cream cheese?
When would be the best time to serve the Triple-Treat Sandwich Loaf?
Would you rather eat Triple-Treat Sandwich Loaf with a fork or with your hands?

Tasty Roll-Ups

Ingredients:

8 thin slices luncheon meat (square)
4 ounces whipped cream cheese
1 teaspoon grated onion
¼ teaspoon Worcestershire sauce

Utensils:

grater
measuring spoons
mixing spoon
paring knife
serving plate
small mixing bowl
spatula to scrape bowl
table knife
toothpicks

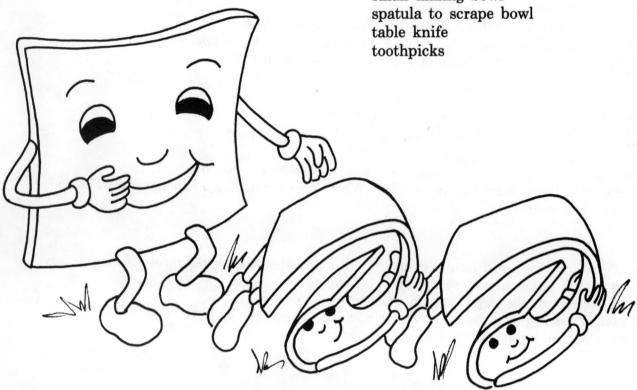

Directions:

1. Stir the cream cheese, onion, and Worcestershire sauce together in the mixing bowl.

2. Spread this mixture on one side of each meat slice.

3. Roll each meat slice into a tight roll.

4. Cut each meat roll into three equal pieces.

5. Stick one toothpick into each piece to hold it together.

6. Arrange on a plate.

7. Serve with pride!

Tasty Roll-Ups

Vocabulary:

Nouns	*Verbs*	*Modifiers*
cream cheese	cut	dull
grater	grate	equal
luncheon meat	measure	grated
measuring spoon	pour	leftover
mixture	roll up	sharp
onion	scrape	thin
paring knife	slice	thirds
spatula	spread	tight
toothpick	stick	whipped
Worcestershire sauce		

Activities:

Pass the onion around before it is peeled and cut. Discuss the texture of the onion skin. Then, cut the onion in half. Have the children smell the fresh onion. Discuss what they smell, and how the onion affects their eyes.

Have the children taste each ingredient and tell how it tastes. Then, ask whether each ingredient tastes good by itself.

Discuss safety tips for using a paring knife and a grater. Show how to hold each one. Talk about what to do if you cut yourself by mistake while using a knife or a grater.

Have the children predict how many toothpicks will be needed for each meat slice since each slice will be cut into thirds.

Zesty Extras:

Tasty Roll-Ups

Blooming Questions:

Knowledge

What ingredients do we use for this recipe?
  meat slices, cream cheese, onion, and Worcestershire sauce
What do we need to do to the onion before we can use it in this recipe? *grate it*
What do we use to spread the cream cheese? *knife*
How does a paring knife feel? *sharp*

Comprehension

Tell how we made Tasty Roll-Ups. *See the recipe.*
Describe what a Tasty Roll-Up looks like.
  two colors, rolled up like a cinnamon roll, has a toothpick in it
Where should we keep leftover Tasty Roll-Ups? Why?
  refrigerator—so they won't spoil
Why did we use square meat slices instead of round ones? *so each roll-up would be the same*

Application

What other foods could we grate? *cheese, cabbage, nuts, etc.*
What other foods do we roll up? *rolls, ice cream cake, etc.*
Why did we only cover one side of each meat slice? *so it's easy to roll up evenly*
Why did we grate the onion instead of chopping it?
  so the pieces are small enough to roll up in the meat easily

Analysis

What meats are luncheon meats made from? *pork, turkey, beef, etc.*
How are onion and Worcestershire sauce alike? *both spicy*
How are they different? *onion is solid food, Worcestershire sauce is a liquid*
Describe cream cheese. What else is like it? *Answers will vary.*

Synthesis

What could we use instead of cream cheese to make this recipe? *cheese spread*
What ingredients could we add to this recipe? *chopped nuts, chopped celery, dill, etc.*
Let's invent a whole new roll-up recipe, but this time, let's make a dessert. *Answers will vary.*

Evaluation

What is the easiest part of making Tasty Roll-Ups?
What is the hardest part?
Are Tasty Roll-Ups healthy food to eat?
Are Tasty Roll-Ups a good party food?

Cantaloupe Fruit Bowl

Ingredients:

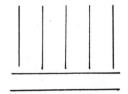

Utensils:

1 whole cantaloupe
1 cup green grapes
1 cup strawberries
vanilla ice cream (optional)

measuring cup
paring knife
small mixing bowl
spoon or melon ball scoop
spoons for tossing

Directions:

1. Cut the cantaloupe in half and remove the seeds.

2. Scoop out the fruit of the cantaloupe in small pieces. Put the pieces in the mixing bowl.

3. After washing, remove the stems from the strawberries.

4. Cut the strawberries into quarters and put them in the mixing bowl.

5. Wash the grapes. Cut them in half and put them in the mixing bowl.

6. Toss the fruit together.

7. Put the mixed fruit into the scooped-out cantaloupe halves.

8. Chill and serve. For a special treat, serve with one scoop of vanilla ice cream on top. Yummy!

Cantaloupe Fruit Bowl

Vocabulary:

Nouns	Verbs	Modifiers
cantaloupe	chill	half
fruit	cut	quarters
grapes	measure	rough
measuring cup	mix	sharp
melon	remove	smooth
melon ball scoop	scoop	whole
paring knife	serve	
rind	toss	
seeds		
spoon		
stems		
strawberries		

Activities:

Pass the melon around before it is cut. Discuss the texture of the rind. Look at the stem end. Talk about other fruits that have stems. Then, cut the melon in half. Have the children look at the seeds and smell the cantaloupe. Have them remove the seeds and feel the membrane around the seeds. Then, discard the seeds.

Have the children examine each ingredient. Ask how each ingredient looks and feels. Then, ask which one is heavier and rougher to touch. Ask which ingredients can be eaten and which ones have rind or skin that shouldn't be eaten.

Pass a strawberry and grape around before they are cut. Again, discuss the texture of the skin. Cut the grape and the strawberry open. Have the children look at the inside of each one. Talk about how they are alike and different.

Have the children predict which fruits will taste sweet.

Zesty Extras:

Cantaloupe Fruit Bowl

Blooming Questions:

Knowledge

What is the name of this recipe? *Cantaloupe Fruit Bowl*
What fruits did we use to make a Cantaloupe Fruit Bowl? *cantaloupe, grapes, and strawberries*
What can we use to get the fruit out of the cantaloupe? *melon ball scoop, spoon*
What do we use to cut the cantaloupe? *paring knife*

Comprehension

Tell how the rind of the cantaloupe feels. *rough, bumpy, coarse*
Should you eat the rind of a cantaloupe? *no*
Do strawberries have smooth skin? *no*
Why did we cut up the fruit? *so it's easier to eat*

Application

What other fruit could we put in the cantaloupe bowl? *bananas, blueberries, kiwi, peaches, etc.*
What else could we use the melon ball scoop for? *watermelon, ice cream, butter, etc.*
What other fruits could we use to make a bowl for fruit? *pineapple, watermelon, grapefruit*

Analysis

How are purple grapes and green grapes alike? *both grapes*
How are they different? *color — purple grapes often have seeds*
What would we have to do if we wanted to use purple grapes? *Take the seeds out.*
How are cantaloupe and watermelon alike? *both melons*
How are they different?
    color — cantaloupe seeds are all in the center, but watermelon seeds are throughout the fruit

Synthesis

We made a fruit bowl. How could we make a vegetable bowl? *Answers will vary.*
Suppose we want only yellow or red fruits. How would we change the recipe?
    Answers will vary.
What would be another good name for this recipe? *Answers will vary.*

Evaluation

Is a Cantaloupe Fruit Bowl a nutritious food to eat?
Would the fruit bowl taste better chilled or heated?
Which way do you prefer eating Cantaloupe Fruit Bowl, with or without ice cream on top?

Deviled Eggs

Ingredients:

6 hard-boiled eggs
2 teaspoons sweet pickle relish
2 tablespoons mayonnaise
1 tablespoon mustard
1 teaspoon minced onion
green olives
salt and pepper

Utensils:

fork
measuring spoons
mixing bowl
paring knife
serving plate
small spoon

Directions:

1. Peel the eggs. Cut them in half lengthwise.

2. Remove the yolks and put them in the mixing bowl. Set the whites aside.

3. Mash the cooked yolks with a fork.

4. Cut the olives into small pieces.

5. Mix all the ingredients until they are well-blended.

6. Use a small spoon to fill the hollowed-out section of each egg white with the yolk mixture.

7. Arrange the stuffed eggs on a plate.

8. Serve. Enjoy the compliments!

Deviled Eggs

Vocabulary:

Nouns	Verbs	Modifiers
eggshell	arrange	hard-boiled
mayonnaise	blend	hollowed-out
mixture	crack	lengthwise
mustard	cut	minced
olives	mash	slippery
onion	mix	soft
pickle relish	peel	stuffed
seasoning	remove	sweet
whites		tart
yolk		

Activities:

Pass the hard-boiled eggs around before they are peeled. Demonstrate how to crack and peel an egg. Have the children look at the uncracked egg and the cracked egg. Discuss how they look and feel.

Discuss how uncooked eggs usually look and feel when they come out of the shell. Discuss the similarities and differences between hard-boiled and soft-boiled eggs.

Have the children experiment with various ways of cutting the eggs in half. Which way do they think works best for this recipe?

Allow the children to smell and taste each ingredient before it is added to the mixture. Talk about differences in taste and appearance.

Zesty Extras:

Deviled Eggs

Blooming Questions:

Knowledge

What are we making? *deviled eggs*
What do we need to do to the eggshells before we peel them? *crack them*
What two green ingredients are we using? *olives, relish*
Where will we put the ingredients to mix them? *in a bowl*

Comprehension

Where should we keep the leftover deviled eggs? Why? *refrigerator—so they won't spoil*
Tell me how we made deviled eggs. *See the recipe.*
Does mayonnaise have eggs in it? *yes*
Is mustard a seasoning? *yes*

Application

What happens when you cook an egg? *It gets hard.*
Can you eat an uncooked egg? Why or why not? *no—it's not good for you, tastes bad*
What else could we make with hard-boiled eggs? *tuna salad, egg salad, potato salad*

Analysis

Why do we use seasonings in deviled eggs? *to add flavor*
Why do we take the yolks out of the eggs? *to add seasonings*
How many halves are in each egg? *two*
Why do we use mayonnaise in the mixture? *to add flavor and to hold the mixture together*

Synthesis

What would happen if we chopped up all of the ingredients and mixed them together?
  We wouldn't have any part to stuff; we'd have egg salad.
What could we use the cracked eggshells for? *Answers will vary, but may include artwork.*
Plan a picnic menu that includes deviled eggs. Make it special! *Answers will vary.*

Evaluation

Are eggs good food for all people?
Are there ingredients in this recipe you would rather leave out?
In your opinion, is "Deviled Eggs" a good name for this recipe?

Celery Boats

Ingredients:

celery stalks
cheese spread

Utensils:

paper towels
paring knife
plate
small spreading knife
vegetable brush

Directions:

1. Wash the celery with the vegetable brush.

2. Cut off the leaves and trim ¼ inch off the top and bottom of each stalk.

3. Dry each stalk with a paper towel.

4. Cut each stalk into 3 equal pieces.

5. Spread cheese spread on each celery piece.

6. Arrange the stuffed celery on a plate.

7. Serve for a crunchy treat!

Celery Boats

Vocabulary:

Nouns	Verbs	Modifiers
celery stalk	cut	rough
cheese spread	fill	sharp
leaves	serve	small
paring knife	spread	smooth
stem	stuff	
strings		
top		
vegetable		
ridges		
thirds		

Activities:

Discuss how celery grows and that the bottom is flat because it was cut from its stalk. Discuss the parts of the stalk, the leaves, the top, and the strings.

Discuss the rough texture and ridges on the outside of each stalk. As you break off a stalk, allow each child to see the shape of the stalk from the bottom to the top. Discuss the depth of the hollow part and how natural it is to hold stuffing.

Discuss the texture of the stuffings and other ingredients that could be used to make this recipe.

Zesty Extras:

Celery Boats

Blooming Questions:

Knowledge

What are we making? *Celery Boats*
What stuffing are we using in the celery? *cheese spread*
What utensil do we use to spread the cheese spread? *knife*
Is a celery stalk flat? *no*

Comprehension

Where do we buy celery? *in the fresh produce section at the grocery store*
Is celery a vegetable or a fruit? *vegetable*
Where do we keep celery to keep it fresh? *refrigerator*
Tell the steps to make Celery Boats. *See the recipe.*

Application

What other food could we stuff? *turkey, pork chop, doughnut, cabbage, etc.*
What other vegetable could we cut in thirds to eat? *carrots, corn on the cob, cucumber, etc.*
What might happen if we didn't cut the celery into small pieces? *It might be awkward to eat.*

Analysis

Where does cheese come from? *cream from cows*
How are cheese spread and peanut butter alike? *both spreads, both have protein*
How are they different? *peanut butter is made from peanuts, cheese spread is a dairy product*

Synthesis

Think of some other things that could be added to the cheese spread before the celery is filled.
  nuts, celery, bacon bits
Think of another recipe to use celery in. *Answers will vary.*
How could we garnish, or decorate, a plate of Celery Boats to make it special?
  parsley, tomato wedges, etc.

Evaluation

Which is healthier, cheese spread or peanut butter?
Which looks prettier on a tray, celery stuffed with peanut butter, cream cheese, or cheese spread?
Would you like a celery sandwich made with two Celery Boats?

Refrigerator Pickles

Ingredients:

2 tablespoons onion flakes
½ teaspoon diced parsley
4 teaspoons sugar
2 teaspoons salt
¼ teaspoon pepper
2 teaspoons celery seed
¾ cup vinegar
¼ cup water
2 tablespoons lemon juice
fresh cucumbers

Utensils:

larged mixing bowl
measuing cup
measuring spoons
paring knife
pint-sized glass jars with tight-fitting lids

Directions:

1. Wash the cucumbers, but don't peel off the skin.

2. Cut the cucumbers into slices.

3. Put the cucumber slices into the jars.

4. Mix all the other ingredients together.

5. Pour the liquid mixture into the jars with the cucumber slices.

6. Put the jars in the refrigerator for four days.

7. Serve for a tasty treat!

Refrigerator Pickles

Vocabulary:

Nouns	Verbs	Modifiers
celery seed	cut	about
cucumbers	mix	approximately
flakes	peel	diced
jars	pour	pint-sized
lemon juice	screw	tight-fitting
lid		
liquid		
parsley		
seasonings		
vinegar		

Activities:

As you slice the cucumbers, discuss the size and why all the slices should be about the same thickness. Discuss the terms *approximately* and *about*.

Talk about the rind or skin on a cucumber and the fact that you don't need to peel it for this recipe. Compare it to other vegetables that do or do not need peeling.

Have the children taste the cucumbers, the liquid mixture, and the finished pickles. Ask them to describe the different tastes.

Have commercial pickles available to taste and compare with the pickles the children have made. Talk about the other pickled foods.

Zesty Extras:

Refrigerator Pickles

Blooming Questions:

Knowledge

What is the name of this recipe? *Refrigerator Pickles*
What vegetable do we use to make pickles? *cucumbers*
Do we slice or dice the cucumber? *slice*

Comprehension

Tell me how to make Refrigerator Pickles. *See the recipe.*
Do we peel the cucumbers? *no*
What is the container for the pickles made of? *glass*
When can we eat the pickles? *after four days*

Application

What other vegetables can we peel? *carrots, potatoes, squash*
What other foods do we cover with vinegar? *pickled herring, pickled cauliflower, salad*
Why do we slice the cucumbers instead of grating them?
    We want to make pickles, not relish. Grating would make them too fine.

Analysis

Where do cucumbers come from? *a plant in the garden*
How are celery seed and pepper alike? *both are black seasonings*
How are they different? *taste*
Which ingredients in this recipe are liquids? *vinegar, lemon juice, and water*

Synthesis

What could we use instead of cucumbers in this recipe? *summer squash, zucchini*
What other seasonings could we use in this recipe? *garlic, celery salt, or sugar*
Predict what would happen if we left the pickles in the refrigerator for only one hour.
    They wouldn't have as much flavor.

Evaluation

Which kind of pickles do you like better, the kind you make at home or the kind you buy at
    the store?
Is it cheaper to make pickles or buy them?
Should pickles always be included on a relish tray?
What foods do you like best with pickles?

64

Cranberry Carnival

Ingredients:

2 stalks of celery
1 orange
1 cup water
2 cups whole cranberries
1 cup sugar
¼ cup pecan pieces

Utensils:

paring knife
mixing bowl
electric blender
small jars with tight-fitting lids
measuring cup

Directions:

1. Cut the celery into small pieces.

2. Cut the orange into small sections, leaving the peel on.

3. Put the celery, the orange, and the water into the blender. Blend at medium speed until the celery and orange are finely chopped.

4. Add ½ cup of cranberries to the mixture in the blender.

5. Blend at medium speed until the cranberries are chopped.

6. Repeat steps 4 and 5 until all the cranberries are chopped.

7. Pour this relish into a bowl. Stir the sugar and pecans into the mixture.

8. Put the relish into the jars and refrigerate. Serve within two weeks.

Cranberry Carnival

Vocabulary:

Nouns	*Verbs*	*Modifiers*
blender	blend	finely
bog	chop	medium
bowl	pour	sharp
celery	refrigerate	small
cranberries	repeat	sour
cup	serve	tart
jars	stir	tight-fitting
orange		water-logged
pecans		
relish		
sections		
speed		

Activities:

Discuss the texture, shape and size of the celery, cranberries, and orange before they are cut or chopped in the blender. Have the children smell each before and after it is cut.

Taste the ingredients and discuss which one is tart, or sour.

Discuss the reason for chopping only ½ cup of the cranberries at a time. Also, discuss the reason for using a blender instead of just chopping the ingredients.

Talk with the children about where cranberries grow (in wet areas of land called *bogs*) and the most popular holidays when cranberry relish might be on the table at home. Talk about how cranberries were used for dye by the settlers.

Zesty Extras:

Cranberry Carnival

Blooming Questions:

Knowledge

What are we making? *Cranberry Carnival*
Where do cranberries grow? *in wet areas called* bogs
On what holidays do we usually have cranberry relish? *Thanksgiving, Christmas*
How do cranberries taste? *tart or sour*

Comprehension

Tell how we made Cranberry Carnival. *See the recipe.*
Describe what we do with the blender. *use it to chop or blend some ingredients*
Describe what a cranberry looks like. *red outside, white inside; small; round*
What does *tart* mean? *sour*

Application

What other foods are tart or sour? *cherries, lemons, grapefruit*
What other foods could we chop in the blender? *onions, apples, peppers, carrots*
What other foods do we serve at Thanksgiving? *turkey, stuffing, pumpkin pie, etc.*

Analysis

How are cranberries and oranges alike? *both fruit, both round*
How are they different?
  cranberries grow on a bush, oranges grow on trees; cranberries have skin, oranges have peel
Why do we put water in the blender with some of the ingredients?
  so food doesn't stick together and gets chopped more evenly

Synthesis

What would happen if you left the cranberry mixture in the blender for five minutes?
  It would be too finely chopped.
What could we use instead of the blender for this recipe? *food processor*
Think of another way you could use cranberries. *Answers will vary.*
What would be another good name for this recipe? *Answers will vary.*

Evaluation

Do you like the taste of cranberries?
How do you think cranberries taste best?
What did you like about making this recipe?
Would the cranberry mixture taste all right if you forgot some of the ingredients?

Ready-to-Go Snack

Ingredients:

½ pound raw, unsalted sunflower seeds
¼ pound unsalted whole almonds
½ cup carob chips
1 cup raisins

Utensils:

measuring cup
mixing bowl
spoons for tossing

Directions:

1. Put all of the ingredients into the mixing bowl.

2. Use two spoons to toss the ingredients together.

3. Serve as a snack. It's ready to go anytime, anywhere.

68

Ready-to-Go Snack

Vocabulary:

Nouns	Verbs	Modifiers
almonds	measure	one-fourth
carob chips	mix	one-half
pound	serve	raw
raisins	stir	unsalted
snack	toss	whole
sunflower seeds		

Activities:

Discuss the texture, shape and size of the sunflower seeds, the almonds, the carob chips, and the raisins. Have the children feel, smell and taste each one individually.

Discuss the difference in weight between ½ pound and ¼ pound. Compare the differences in weight by the amount of nuts and sunflower seeds.

Talk about the advantages of tossing the ingredients in this recipe rather than stirring, mixing, or blending them.

Carob is a substitute for chocolate in many recipes. Let the children compare the taste of carob chips and chocolate chips. Then, ask which chips they prefer.

Zesty Extras:

Ready-to-Go Snack

Blooming Questions:

Knowledge

What are we making? *Ready-to-Go Snack*
What are the ingredients we need? *See the recipe.*
What utensil do we use for tossing? *spoons*

Comprehension

Tell how we made the Ready-to-Go Snack. *See the recipe.*
Where do sunflower seeds come from? *sunflowers*
What does *raw* mean? *not cooked*

Application

What other food does carob remind you of? *chocolate chips*
What would happen if we mixed this recipe with a blender?
  It would be harder to eat because the pieces would be smaller.
What other foods are for snacks? *fruits, pretzels, vegetables, potato chips, etc.*

Analysis

How are carob and chocolate chips alike? *both look alike, have same size and texture*
How are they different? *taste*
How many people will our snack serve? *about 10-15 people*

Synthesis

How are carob chips like raisins?
  both are sweet, both can go in snacks, both are healthful food
Make up a new ingredient that could be used instead of carob. *Answers will vary.*
Make up a TV ad to sell Ready-to-Go Snack in small boxes. *Answers will vary.*

Evaluation

Would this snack give you lots of energy?
Would this snack be a good gift to give to someone?
Which ingredients do you like best in this recipe? Draw your favorite place to eat Ready-to-Go
  Snack.
Is "Ready-to-Go" a good name for this snack?

Fruit-Nut Jamboree

Ingredients:

1 tablespoon grated orange peel
1 cup raisins
¼ cup dried prunes, chopped
¼ cup dried apricots, chopped
¼ cup orange juice
¼ cup shredded coconut
¼ cup pecan or walnut pieces
butter or margarine

Utensils:

grater
large mixing bowl
measuring cup
measuring spoons
serving plate
paring knife
spoons for tossing
8″ × 8″ glass dish

Directions:

1. Put all of the ingredients into the large mixing bowl.

2. Toss the ingredients using two spoons.

3. Butter the glass dish. Press the mixture into the buttered dish.

4. Cut the mixture into small individual servings or bars. Leave the bars in a cool place for 24 hours.

5. After 24 hours, remove individual servings from the dish and arrange them on a serving plate.

6. Serve for a tempting treat!

Fruit-Nut Jamboree

Vocabulary:

Nouns	*Verbs*	*Modifiers*
apricots	butter	cool
bars	cut	dried
grater	grate	grated
orange	press	individual
orange juice	remove	shredded
pecan		square
pieces		
prunes		
raisins		
scale		
servings		
walnut		

Activities:

Pass an orange around before it is grated. Discuss the texture and smell of the peel. Discuss what is happening as the peel is grated. Point out how much of the peel was grated to make one tablespoon. Let the children smell the grated peel.

Measure all of the ingredients that require ¼ cup. Put each one in an identical container. Then, use a kitchen scale to compare the weight difference of the various ingredients.

Discuss the reason for buttering the dish before adding the mixture. Mention other times we butter a pan or casserole dish.

Discuss what happens to the mixture after you toss it and then how it changes in appearance after it is pressed into the dish. See if the children can figure out what makes the mixture stick together.

Ask the children to describe the appearance of the mixture immediately after it is put into the dish and again after the 24-hour waiting period. Discuss any changes they see.

Zesty Extras:

Fruit-Nut Jamboree

Blooming Questions:

Knowledge

Name the ingredients we use for this recipe. *See the recipe.*
What must we do with each ingredient before we add it? *measure it*
What utensil do we use to grate the orange peel? *grater*

Comprehension

Show how we made the grated orange peel. *child demonstrates grating an orange*
Show how we cut the mixture into bars. *child demonstrates cutting into bars*
Are dried fruits juicy? *no*

Application

What would happen if we forgot the orange juice?
  The ingredients wouldn't stick together because they would be too dry.
What might happen if we put in too much orange juice?
  The ingredients would be too wet and sticky.
What would happen if we forgot the coconut? *It would taste different.*
Tell me all the kinds of nuts you can think of. *walnuts, pecans, peanuts, cashews, almonds, etc.*

Analysis

How are prunes and apricots alike? *both are fruit, both taste sweet, both have pits*
How are they different? *prunes are dark, apricots are light*
Which ingredient makes the mixture juicy? *orange juice*
Which ingredient is made from plums? *prunes*

Synthesis

What would you do if you had to serve this recipe to three hundred people? Tell how you
  would do it. *Answers will vary.*
What kind of kitchen would you set up to take care of this large order? *Answers will vary.*
How could we change this recipe to make it a complete breakfast? *Answers will vary.*

Evaluation

Would this be a good snack to serve to your friends after school?
Would this snack be healthier than a brownie?
Which ingredients do you like best?
Which ingredients would you rather leave out of this recipe?

Graham Cracker Piecrust

Ingredients:

1 package graham crackers
¼ cup sugar
4 tablepoons melted butter or margarine

Utensils:

measuring cup
mixing bowl
plastic bag (8″ × 11″)
rolling pin
9″ pie pan

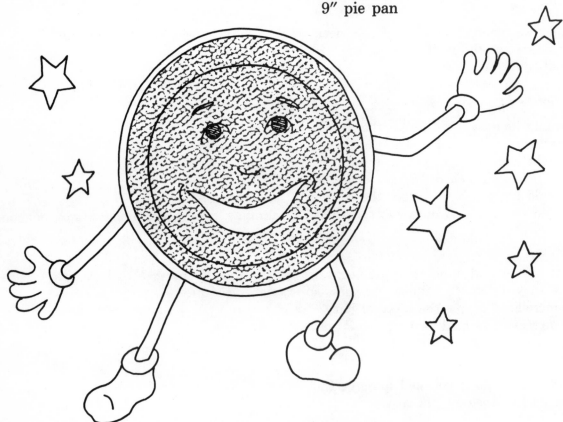

Directions:

1. Put the graham crackers into the plastic bag and fasten the top.

2. Flatten the crackers with the rolling pin. Continue to crush them until they are fine crumbs.

3. Pour the cracker crumbs, the sugar, and the melted butter into the mixing bowl.

4. Mix by hand until the crumbs stick together.

5. Put the mixture into the pie pan. Use your fingers to press the mixture to the bottom and sides of the pan evenly.

6. Chill the piecrust for one hour before adding pie filling.

Graham Cracker Piecrust

Vocabulary:

Nouns	Verbs	Modifiers
crumbs	chill	evenly
graham cracker	crush	fine
pie filling	fasten	melted
pie pan	flatten	
piecrust	mix by hand	
rolling pin	press	
	stick together	

Activities:

Have the children watch while you melt the butter. Put the butter in a glass cup or bowl and use a candle below to melt the butter, or use a hot plate to melt it. Have the children describe what is happening to the butter as it melts.

Have the children describe what is happening to the graham crackers as they are being crushed. Discuss the differences in texture and appearance between the whole crackers and the crumbs.

As the children stir the crumb mixture, have them describe how the mixture looks and what is happening to it. Then, have them tell how the mixture feels as they press it into the pie pan.

Once the piecrust is chilled, show it to the children. Ask them to describe any differences they notice in the way the piecrust looks, feels, and smells after it has been chilled.

Zesty Extras:

Graham Cracker Piecrust

Blooming Questions:

Knowledge

What ingredients do we need for this recipe? *See the recipe.*
What do we need to do to the butter before we can use it? *Melt it.*
What do we use to crush the graham crackers? *rolling pin*
What do we put the piecrust mixture into? *a pie pan*

Comprehension

Describe how to make graham cracker piecrust. *See the recipe.*
Why do we use a bag when we crush the graham crackers? *so they won't make a mess*
Is this true? We use a knife to crush the graham crackers. *no — We use a rolling pin.*
Where do we put the piecrust to chill? *in the refrigerator*

Application

Fix this silly sentence. We put cake filling in a piecrust. *We put pie filling in a piecrust.*
What other foods could we crush into crumbs? *bread, soda crackers, cookies*
What else could we use to crush the graham crackers? *meat tenderizer, wooden spoon*
What would happen if we used twice as much melted butter? *The crust wouldn't hold its shape.*

Analysis

How is graham cracker piecrust like regular piecrust? *shape*
How is it different? *taste*
We used graham crackers and butter to make this piecrust. What else did we add? *sugar*
Which did we do to the crackers first, mix them or crush them? *crush them*
What could we use instead of sugar to sweeten the piecrust? *honey*

Synthesis

What kinds of pie fillings could we put into the piecrust? *ice cream, pudding, etc.*
Imagine you could design a new shape for pies. Draw your shape and name your invention.
  Make it creative! *Answers will vary.*
Imagine a piecrust made out of something else crunchy. What would you use?
  cookies, pretzels, other crackers

Evaluation

Tell which kind of piecrust you like better, graham cracker piecrust or regular (pastry) piecrust.
Which parts of this recipe are easiest to do with your fingers?
What's the hardest part about making this recipe?
Which part is the most fun to do?

Yummy Yogurt Pie

Ingredients:

2 small containers of fruit-flavored yogurt
1 container of non-dairy whipped topping
1 graham cracker piecrust

Utensils:

mixing bowl
spatula

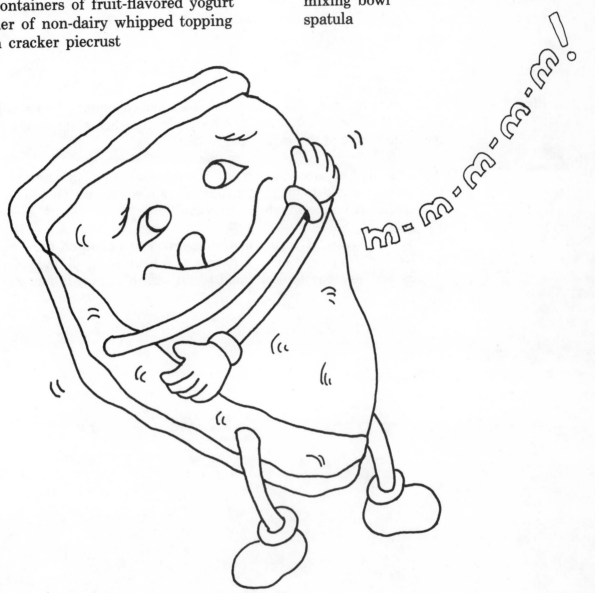

Directions:

1. Put the yogurt and the non-dairy whipped topping into the mixing bowl.

2. Using a spatula, fold these ingredients together gently.

3. Pour the mixture into the graham cracker piecrust.

4. Chill the pie for at least four hours before serving.

Yummy Yogurt Pie

Vocabulary:

Nouns	Verbs	Modifiers
piecrust	chill	non-dairy
spatula	fold	whipped
topping	pour	
yogurt		

Activities:

Let the children taste the yogurt and the whipped topping individually. Then, let them taste the mixture after these ingredients are folded together. Have them compare the tastes.

Discuss the folding procedure during the process. Demonstrate the difference between stirring and folding. Mention other mixtures we fold, such as beaten egg whites or flavoring in whipped cream.

Have several flavors of yogurt available. Have the children taste each flavor. Then, let the group vote on one flavor, or substitute small, individual piecrusts and give one to each child to fill with her favorite flavor.

Zesty Extras:

Yummy Yogurt Pie

Blooming Questions:

Knowledge

What ingredients do we need to make this pie? *See the recipe.*
What kind of piecrust do we use? *graham cracker*
What do we do to mix the yogurt and the whipped topping together? *fold it*

Comprehension

Tell how we know when the yogurt and the whipped topping are mixed well enough.
 It's all the same color.
Where do we keep foods like yogurt and whipped topping? *refrigerator*
Is this true? Fruit-flavored yogurt is always white. *no*
Tell how to make Yummy Yogurt Pie. *See the recipe.*

Application

We buy yogurt and whipped topping in cartons. What other foods come in cartons?
 cole slaw, cottage cheese, ice cream, etc.
We folded the yogurt and the whipped topping. What other mixtures do we fold?
 egg whites, whipped cream
Name all the fruits you could add to yogurt. *Answers will vary.*

Analysis

Which ingredients would you find in the refrigerator? *yogurt, non-dairy whipped topping*
What is yogurt made from? *milk*
What does *non-dairy* mean? *made without any dairy products*

Synthesis

How are yogurt and whipped topping alike? *texture*
How are they different? *taste*
What would you add to this recipe to make it a special birthday party pie? Draw your
 creation. *Answers will vary.*
If you didn't have any piecrust, how could you serve this recipe?
 ice cream cone, cupcake liner, pudding dish

Evaluation

Which is your favorite yogurt flavor?
Which do you like better, fruit-flavored yogurt or ice cream?
Would Yummy Yogurt Pie be a good dessert to take on a picnic?